Slippage

BK Poems

Slippage

BK Poems

Providence, RI
2016

Copyright © 2016 by Baruch Kirschenbaum

All rights reserved. No part of this book may be reproduced or transmitted in any form or by any means whatsoever without express written permission from the author, except in the case of brief quotations embodied in critical articles and reviews. Please refer all pertinent questions to the author.

Cover drawing: Emily Hass
Author portrait: Edward M. Brown

Permission to adapt descriptive text into poem "Li Jun Lai Palimpsest" granted by artist Li Jun Lai.

This book was edited and designed by Michael Gnat.

PUBLISHER'S CATALOGING-IN-PUBLICATION DATA
Names: Kirschenbaum, Baruch David, 1931–, author.
Title: Slippage : BK Poems.
Description: Providence, RI: [s.n.], 2016.
Identifiers: ISBN 978-0-692-76245-5
Subjects: LCSH Poetry. | American poetry. | BISAC POETRY / American / General.
Classification: LCC PS3611.I772 S55 2016 | DDC 811.6—dc23

This collection of poems is dedicated to EG, *without whom these poems would never have been written, and to* MG, *without whom they never would have seen the light of day.*

I think about the poems I write as brief essays in poetic form on experiences and observations and, more abstractly, on the nature of things as I see them. In that sense, my poems are more thought poems than what are referred to as "Language poems"—which is not to suggest that there is no thought in the latter, for clearly there is. I do, however, usually write without punctuation, perhaps to slow the uptake of meaning. More than that there is little to say, except that I hope you will find some virtue and pleasure in these meditations.

—BK

Contents

I

Slippage	3
Shower	5
Islands of Memory	7
Rebels	9
Contretemps	11
Summer Song	13
Daphne	15
Lament/A Love Poem	17
Troubled Dream	19
Complaint	21
Pace Andrew	23
Morning Ablutions	25
Cavafy Dream	27

II

Meditation	31
Strange Entanglements	33
Stone	35
Luxury	37
Prodigal	39
Sleeping Dogs	41
Wisdoms	43
Bowline	45
One by One	47
Night Flight	49
Ode to a Sphinx	51
Beautiful	53

INSCRIBED	55
IT NEVER WAS	57
THE POETIC LINE	61
LI JUN LAI PALIMPSEST	63
UNTO	65

III

DESTINATION	69
TMI	71
DURATION	73
TRUE GRACE	75
TRINITY STONES	77
HERO	79
DOPE	81
EVERY BODY	83
POST OFFICE	85
GRAFFITI	87
BETRAYAL	89

IV

SUMMER SOLSTICE	93
TURF	95
MOSQUITO	97
SYLLOGISM	99
FOR THE BIRDS	101
INDEPENDENCE	103
FOR ROSIE	105
CRUMBS	107
ODE TO BUTTER	109
QUIETUDE	111

Slippage

BK Poems

I

Slippage

Give me a second
it's on the tip of my mind
it will come to me
        but for now more and
        more things will come
        to me than do come to me
lost in the deepening
brambles of the mind
teasing just beyond reach
        and when they do come
        they come with a rush
        of triumph and delight
for the bird's now firmly
in the hand and for the moment
all well-being and faith restored
        like the endings on the
        comic stage all lovers
        paired and all evil undone.

Shower

Stepping
unselfconsciously
naked
out of the shower
reaching
for the dark blue bath towel
to begin
another ordinary day
list already
in mind when in a rush
a dark blue bird
feathered wings
extended
like the great eagle
of Zeus
with a startled Ganymede in grasp
carried me
out and up to a wild peak
in a wild place
and then the day
began

Islands of Memory

Islands of memory
uncharted
in the sea of time
obscured
by ocean mists
and the ebb
and flow
of tides
on which
Crusoe-like to be
washed ashore
and not without some
reservations

Rebels

Two maybe three
insistent black hairs

in a gray white beard
of some duration

rebels—young and angry—
against biological

inevitability
and related systems

god bless 'em

Contretemps

My purpose was
          just to pass
things along from the
               Unmentionable—
with whom I thought
          silly me
you had made arrangements—
             incidentally so
but with a touch of urgency
           all of which
offended your inviolable taste
           for which
apologies in this always brief
            light of ours—OK?

Summer Song

At last I've reached a truly contemplative
camaraderie with the state of nature
not rude unkempt but idyllic with gently
rolling hills and flowering meadows
all sort of wordsworthian without
the peasants or the cow flops

a camaraderie of pleasure enjoyed
from a disengaged distance with
a glass of wine and thou to assuage any guilt for
being so detached a viewer of the scene
for which I abjure any nurturing
responsibility

let the nymphs and shepherds dance
round hill and dale in arcadian games
and let the gods bless them in their
riggishness and forgive my passive reveries
as I delight in knowing they are
surely there in this mind's eye

Daphne

It's not clear
she thought perhaps
she never wanted
not to be caught
in this woodland game
but it is clear
she never wanted
to be rooted in the earth
bereft forever of love

she could she thought
still feel the hot breath
of pursuit so close behind
and the pounding of her
own heart beneath the
imprisoning bark

and knew that for
freedom of desire and
the pleasures of the flesh she
would have offered herself
openly to the startled god
breathless behind her

Lament/A Love Poem

Life's a beast—devouring time
out of hand so we can never even
for an instant have again the moments
of our best selves

Love is time's fool no matter
how much we poetize against
it and that my Sweet is that
for the moment

Troubled Dream

I left them—two of them
there was trouble
I left them in the midst
then it wasn't clear
whom I left in the midst
it could have been
the two of us that I left

there was trouble
that much is clear and
that I left whomever
it was I left in the midst
there was trouble
and will be trouble again
whom will I then leave
how then will I escape

Complaint

It's living makes one a liability
or the accumulation of living as if
liability—not the insurable kind—lies
just around that corner you must
inevitably go round waiting as if
in anticipation of the inevitable
fuckup that seals the deal as though
written (dear Brutus) in our stars
or better—nowadays—in our genes
that clutter those twisted strands
of DNA—or so it sometimes seems

Pace Andrew

I want to kiss you till your ears fly off
love until the cows come home
slowly, slowly
we've world enough and time
until the rooster crows at break of day
and the world ends
slowly, slowly my love

Morning Ablutions

I always thought those
morning ablutions they do
were meant for below the
waist exclusively where those
complex labial parts reside
but as it turns out there's no
such overriding protocol

But that revelation calls
to mind those decades ago
in the postwar Netherlands
when warm water was to be
used only below the waist
for the rest cold would suffice
for austerity and complexion

But if I were to follow that
train of thought—just let it spool
out—it would lead to events in
the rest of my life at that time
to which I'd just as soon not go
at the moment

Cavafy Dream

I want to give myself
        to myself
crowned with desires and
        secret passions
beyond apparent need
or capacity at this
late date without fear of fear
        or fear of loss
or discovery

II

Meditation

there must be a thousand poems even
a thousand thousand even a thousand
to the 10th power about the mysticism
of the shower where

in god's good graces blessed with
hot water enough we may enter a state
of meditation letting the mind go where
the mind will go

without intersession as naked we soap
down and vacantly rinse off to prepare for
the ordinary day but feeling just a little as
though touched by revelation

Strange Entanglements

Can it be as now apparently
confirmed
that across the infinity of Einsteinian
spacetime
like particles entangle like
as though
by the mystery of sympathetic
magic
that freed the great aurochs
of Lascaux
from their cave walls to the mean
realities
of Paleolithic life
and which causality we thought
we long ago
left behind to shamanistic
practices

Stone

There is nothing that's set
in stone except the stone
and even that's not set
in stone it will shatter
and flow in the molten
convulsions of the earth
transmogrified into
yet other stone that's not
set in stone

Luxury

There's a certain luxury
in self-deprivation
it sets the ground for
the weeping pleasure
of feeling sorry for oneself
wrapping us around like
a familiar blanket
deepening the pleasures
of isolation as it must
have been for the desert
fathers cultivating deprivation's
perverse pleasures
of denial for the promise
of eternal salvation
in masochistic bliss

Prodigal

    Sending love to you and my dad
(given in the lower case—an index of easy familiarity)
    and please give Lily-Bee (the tabby cat) a pat for me
the closing of an incidental e-mail from JD
    who just the other night I referred to as my prodigal child
who never knew what she really wanted
    leading her like the parable's younger son into the wild
and exciting parts of the world where the demons
    of profligacy thrive and law and institutions
follow with the wrenching of souls, but she who was lost
    is found again and embraced
as Rembrandt's aged father kneels to embrace
    his prodigal's return

Sleeping Dogs

Like they say
        let sleeping dogs lie
meaning that
        the past reinvigorated
will only mean
        trouble and heartache
as what was
        in all its complexities
returns with
        a deeper bite and
the threat
        of more blood to spill
let them lie I say

Wisdoms

No doubt I will face the music
when I cross that bridge to which
I will most certainly come and will
need no longer count my chickens
before or after or wonder whether
they'll come home to roost or if a
stitch in time really does save nine
determined not by any accounting
but by rhyme alone or whether in
reality a penny saved is a penny
earned in a world where those who
hesitate are lost and where even
angels fear to tread and never let
a camel get its nose under the tent
or pass through the eye of a needle

Bowline

There's a mnemonic for tying a standard bowline—
one of the world's great working knots
      with which you can make a loop
      at the end of a line that will not slip—
      the stronger the pull the tighter the hold.

The mnemonic goes: the squirrel comes out of its hole,
goes around the tree and back in its hole
      the hole being a small loop made
      in the standing end—that part of the line
      that remains inactive in tying a knot.

In making the small loop leave in the working end
of the line—as opposed to the standing end—enough
      length to make the end loop which
      you desired in tying the bowline
      to be begin with—remember.

With the small loop (placed as given above) the standing
end of the line must be behind the loop—that's crucial—
      behind not in front of the small
      loop or you'll be left dangling
      with no place to go.

So the squirrel—the working end of the line forming
the end loop—comes out of its hole—the small loop—
        goes around the tree—the standing end
        of the line behind the small loop—
        to check things out as squirrels will.

And then goes immediately back in its hole—the small loop
again—but in reverse—to settle in its comfort and safety
        perhaps to write more poems
        to send out into the world or
        sulk over a lost love.

Tighten and there's the bowline in all its elegant simplicity—
one coil cinching the lines that form the end loop
        that will not slip no matter how
        strong the pull unless under mega
        stress the line itself as in life snaps
        and what was secured is lost—oh lost.

One by One

One by one they fall like
windfalls in the orchard
first this complaint (minor)
then that (not so minor)
then the appointments
the tests the imagings
then the poisons (minor)
and poisons (not so minor)
but still they fall one by one
like windfalls in the orchard
one less e-mail address
one more deletion as the
address book grows
thinner adding absence
to absence
deepening the toll
                but ask not for whom....

Night Flight

Wing tip strobe lights
flash in the palpable
blackness of the night
then—trust reduced—
the slow decent below
the clouds with ganglia
of clustered lights spread-
ing from point to point
to point as we bank above
cities for a still distant
landing and in this moment
on the dark side of the
earth how sad our efforts
seem against the pervading
blackness of the night and
how great the unseen sun
that will bring it all to light

Ode to a Sphinx

After all these years
of personal
association I still don't
understand my
bowels which in the end
seem to have
a mind of their own when
it comes to relating
cause to effect predictably
as if to maintain their
independency
even as we enjoy a
codependency
or better still a *folie à deux*
served by a
sensitive sphincter privy to
its own intentions

Beautiful

What happened to my beautiful body
never really beautiful in fashion's sense
but passing well enough

What happened to my beautiful body
the flesh sags
crepe paper skin wrinkles
and discolors
veins branch out like tributaries of some
unknown delta

what happened to my beautiful body
the skeletal frame
creaks for want of lubrication
as bone grinds on bone
and muscles once willing suffer even
the easy task

what happened to my beautiful body
never really beautiful in fashion's sense
but still passable in my mind's eye
                     and I hope as well in yours

Inscribed

SPQR *Senatus Populusque Romanus*
beneath the streets under foot the great Empire
present just as it was: Cicero and Pompey, Caesar
and Brutus, Anthony and Octavius (the August) with
Livia (the Vengeful) together at their palace in the clear
air of the Palatine above the city, Caligula (the Crazy)
Hadrian, Nero, Titus—et alia—before and after, betogaed
like the marbles lining the halls of the Vatican—
a cast of thousands to which all roads lead
ruling and plotting, getting and spending, living and
killing—*tutto le strade portano a Roma*—with the ruins
of empire jutting out above with sheep grazing in the
shadows of romantic dreams of Piranesian *vedute* the
outward signs of inward dwelling grace—but better yet—
power, wealth beyond imagination, ambition, beauty
and betrayal, love and circuses, Ovid and Catullus,
Virgil and Suetonius all, all in living black and white
alla Fellini as remembered in the mind's eye
SPQR *Sono Pazzi Questi Romani*

It Never Was
(for GM 2010)

It never was the
way they said it was
verdant and green
(don't tell me, I know)
with dominion over all
in lovingkindness for
that brief moment and
then only a dream

of eternal return—still
with signs against the
evil eye and Charon's
coin clenched firmly
in hand as surety
against what might yet
be as this small integrity
of ours is everywhere

threatened not shot
to death bludgeoned
blown apart by IEDs
starved or mangled in

a wreck of twisted steel
and plastic like Warhol's
Saturday night multiples
horn still blaring or

narcotized upon a gurney
unaware of all their
"heroic efforts" or under
some highway underpass
with refuse and mangy
dogs or alone and soiled
in some SRO cheap
hotel in nowheresville

not so far anyway in this
best of all possible worlds
with its strange pathogens—
bacteria, viruses, mutant
cells—lurking everywhere
like the hordes of demons
tormenting Grünewald's
agèd Saint Anthony

to no avail, but closer
than we think with the
drip of intravenous poisons

that promise (maybe) survival
in some double-loaded
refuge with landscaped
grounds and tasteless
food to wait in medicated

euphoria only dimly
aware of the attentions of
underpaid caregivers and
the obligatory visits of
remembered faces that
prepare to meet this face
with spring flowers and
hushed concerns

but might it after all be
other than they said it was—
no green peaceable kingdom
from which to fall—only
the silent empty void
(don't tell me, I know)—
sans everything—that
seals up all the rest.

All's well that ends. . . .

The Poetic Line

Dare I say
>with all regard for the line
that it's not the line, but as with every
>locomotion, the brakes that
slow forward motion and set the
>pace and rhythm of the voyage
and stop us before we go over the cliff
>like Thelma and Louise or
ride the runaway train hurtling down
>the line to episode's end
or offer a poem of infinite extension
>sans breaks to allow for
pause or breath or hesitation
>that release the disarticulation
with which a poem struggles for its life
>and substance
but enough with the poetic line let's talk
>about brakes
or if you'd rather
>breaks

Li Jun Lai Palimpsest
[from a description of the artist's work]

resolution
    sharpness
        roundness

erase/delete/remove

begin. . . . . .overwrite

indistinctness
    movement
        weightness

obscure/hide/cancel

again. . . . . .overwrite

parts aggregate
    combine
        regenerate

annul/override/strike

again.........once more

    unstable wholes
        fall apart
            entropy

bleach/obliterate/trash

again.........end

embodiment
    shadow
        traces of things passed..........

Unto

How gently it is snowing
how gently
Why then the
intimations
of mortality
(yes, I know)
from the sickbed
of only passing
complaint

III

Destination

etaoin shrdlu etaoin etaoin etaoin
shrdlu buried in the city of the archive
archaeology of lost time and shifty
characters error enthroned by fallible fingers
running down the black line of the commonest twelve (lc)
escaping the fiery furnace of Shadrach Meshach and Abednego
to be laid in a cold bed of molten lead by slippage
shards in the lost city of the archive
microfiche digitized etaoin shrdlu recollecting
heroic days of yesteryear for romantic time travelers
searching out the sacred twelve of dada
nonsense of the apostles of the past where they
fell from those selfsame fallible fingers speaking
truth but condemned by fault to etaoin shrdlu
blessed are they for ever and ever
seven two one nine seven eight

TMI

It may be that
I suffer from
the condition
of information
aversion or
more seriously
from information
avoidance or
clinically from
information
anxiety
or simply from
too much TMI
and fear it's
eating my soul
and I can't do
anything about
it

Duration

It's good for the Duration
which used to mean the Duration
of The War after which it would be over
and life and things would get back to
normal and we could once again live
life as it was meant to be lived

without shortages without rationing
without blackouts and air raid drills without
headlights half blacked out without the whole
damned war effort without men in uniform
on the way to overseas and danger without
fear itself that it would never end

but now The War long over we still talk
of the Duration meaning perhaps the end
of time itself or one's own time or at least
the end of a relationship having reached
its proper Duration all of which is nothing
compared to the end of The War

that in those naive times we thought
would come to its unconditional end

and after its Duration we would be reborn
in triumph and innocence as a nation but
that's not quite the way it all worked out
for us
Is it

True Grace

Will I say when it's close to the end
like Bonhoeffer under frightful duress
"I want my life I demand my own life back"

and then the question—all—do I want it
all back or do I get to pick and choose
and would that be a fair deal

or a stacking of the deck to game
the system for a pathological longing
for some idolized reality that

never existed or wouldn't have even
if all things cracked just the way I would
have had them crack even if I knew what

that might be then or now unlike Bonhoeffer
the god-possessed who through belief
knew his game and stood his ground

never to have that or any life returned
on earth—may he rest in grace

Trinity Stones

If you stand in just the right spot
                looking east
you can see in the foreground as in
                the sepia photograph that
hangs on my wall—a gift of long ago—the
                weathered grave stones in
Trinity Church yard worn and slightly off true
                with age and beyond the
towers of Wall Street slicing the sky and
                echoing those old stones as
grave markers yet to come of a bygone
                civilization that
does not hear the whisper of time at its back

Hero

As from an ancient red-figure
amphora he stands tall
muscular alert in white T-shirt
back from the wars
spatula in hand tending
burgers on the gas grill
for the neighbors on the deck
of a Sunday afternoon with
the usual chatter

Was it ever like that for
the famed warriors of Ilium
should he not wander with
Odysseus to expiate the blood lust
or with Aeneas to found a great city
or return to death like Agamemnon
for past sins sword still at side
or like Sarpedon on that great krater
be carried off the field of battle
by sleep and death even as
others prepare for strife

But listen a job is a job
at the Sunday grill or in a blasted
Humvee on the desert floor
halfway around the world
trained and deployed for war
after which there is no normal
only charade as his hand shakes
ever so slightly as he turns back
to the burgers on the grill

Dope

It used to be said
among certain associates
that dope would get you through
times without money better than
money would get you through
times without dope

but that was then when
dope was scarce and sacred
down to stashed roaches and
insanely illegal and from long ago
in the idyllic time
before time
we thought

Every Body

Everybody gets cancer
every body
so it seems when you
look around
when you hear around
every body
everybody innocent
or stained
awaits the judgment
call of MRI
and laboratory test of
every body
and then for everybody
the battle
of the poisons begins for
every body
lined up anonymously
in chairs with
everybody else waiting
for reprieve

Post Office

The Post Office by notice
            cannot accept
replacement checks in settlement
            of any returned
checks—once burned twice shy—
            in modern life as with
Pilgrim and his burden of transgressions
            narrow is the way
and strait the gate if only for the
            US Postal Service
which according to the latest reports
            is on its last
financial legs declared again by those
            who refuse
to recognize it as a moral force in our
            always slipping situation

Graffiti

my flesh has no reality
I can live no longer by thinking

scrawled
above a urinal
with a pencil-drawn
naked torso
head thrown back
arms out stretched
pleading
fists clenched

in kindred spirits
years ago at the same
moment of reverie
the conviction that my
body existed only
to keep my head
off the ground
coraggio poverino

Betrayal

I just learned
by careful reading
that the Japanese
underwear I bought
in New York was
made in China

It's rather good
underwear but still
a disappointment
as if I were sold
a pig in a poke—know
what I mean

I mean if it's really
Japanese—like a
Toyota—shouldn't
it be made in Japan
despite our globalized
economy

it feels different to
have my parts cradled
in something made
in the common image
of the endless Chinese
labor factory

rather than in a
neat Japanese
workshop with white
paper walls with
workers served little
cups of steaming tea

oh silly me
after all underwear
is only underwear
and clichés clichés
in this always shifting
modern world

and wasn't it
only yesterday that
the Japanese were
the enemy savaging
the Chinese in a rush
for greater empire

IV

Summer Solstice

I await the year's summer solstice impatiently
        not for the endless summer
days it promises but for that celestial instant when
        spinning slowly on its tilted
axis the earth reaches its apogee to offer us our
        longest light of day even
as in that instant it begins its slow downward turn
        toward the short white days
of fall which I feel less responsible for wasting
        by conjuring in this mind's eye
the slow axial spinning of the planet revolving around
        the sun in crowded spacetime
        that once we called the heavens

Turf

They fought like cats in the night
the cats Brando and Rosie
in their tiny contested backyard
shattering the air
with screeches as they crouched
on haunches
in hunting mode ready to pounce
but first nonchalantly
to wash as if nothing was up
then another jungle screech
teeth bared only to back
off and walk innocently
away from the face-off but now
that Rosie had to be
put to sleep as they say in the trade
Brando wanders
their contested turf disconsolately
his life seemingly
to have lost its raison d'être
and the old man
has put on some weight or so
it seems

Mosquito

The whack came suddenly
as I was going about my business
it ripped off two legs still twitching
and tore a wing making it impossible
to lift off even if I could with the pain
shooting through my nervous system
and all for a tiny drop of blood which
I never even got anyway as I writhed
to my dismembered end on the back
of a lily-white hand and the exultant
scream—Got 'im!

Syllogism

Cats are not allowed on the counter
you are a cat
therefore you are not allowed on the counter
but cats do not recognize (in either meaning)
syllogistic validity or truth
        still this AM particularly
        there's something about my cat
that I covet as in an instant she springs to the
        countertop
in search of contraband that might be hidden there
        the devil take your syllogism
        with its premises and conclusions
all men are mortal ...

For the Birds

In a backyard rich with birds
    Harvard crimson cardinals
not so gaudy ladies always near
    flashy stealth blue jays black-
capped chickadees and tawny nut
    hatches upside down
digging insects out of the bark of trees
    red-headed woodpeckers
their rhythmic peck peck pecking adding
    a beat to the day

Why is it then in this yard of fancy-dan
    birds my heart goes
out to the little dirt-brown sparrows that
    with concentrated
attention police the ground for crumbs
    left behind by others
of a higher station for these commonest
    of birds who as
biblical gleaners find their survival at the
    edge of plenty

But then again:

I've always been for the under
    dog—the disregarded
of the world—even if not quite the case
    the sparrows it seems
are getting along quite well even on winter-
    frigid days and are
known to have something of a disreputable
    reputation on the street

Independence

Morning Noon
and Night
the days fly by
according to
their own intention
as if I had
nothing to do with it
being just
along for the ride
some times
good some times
not so good
hard to tell in
advance

Morning Noon
and Night
the gray squirrels
scamper up
and down the old
sugar maple
in the backyard
watching I wonder
whether it's true
for them
I think probably
it is.

For Rosie

For Rosie the cat all change bodes no good
and more and more deep in my heart I find myself
in sympathy with her worldview wanting only
that which displays an *evident necessity*—to borrow
a term from Charles Rosen—desiring the exquisite
stasis of things not in their perfection but in all
their imperfections as they are at hand demanding
no attention no fiddling no improvements except
for those small things that always drive us crazy
but my sweet I'm willing to negotiate—go along
to get along as they say—which is more than
I can say for Rosie who without complaint adjusts
to the evident necessity of the always shifting
semblance of things even as they clearly bode no
good for her as they have so painfully this summer

Crumbs

Crumbs
it's always about crumbs
which men seem to shed like water
off a duck's back or seagull droppings
on a clean white boat

Crumbs
which men without
regard to race or sexual orientation
nonchalantly shed on floors
of immaculate kitchens

Crumbs
which men seem to shed simply
by their natures as they move through
life innocent of experience
pace Wm Blake

Crumbs
it's always about crumbs
meanwhile the moon goes 'round
the earth and earth the sun
mea culpa mea maxima culpa

Ode to Butter

Butter
which of all things
in the world
can't be duplicated
it is what
it is with all its
virtues
whether hand churned
between
the knees or industrially
produced
blessed be
whatever genius
of long ago
invented it to whom
we owe
a great salaam
for a gift
worthy of the gods
themselves
with which to short
a confection
fry an egg or comfort
a piece of toast

Quietude

White on white squared revolving
on a white plane

minor key changes from tone to tone
of the gray scale

black on still deeper black just
barely audible

www.ingramcontent.com/pod-product-compliance
Lightning Source LLC
Chambersburg PA
CBHW032044290426
44110CB00012B/941